I can draw animals

Ray Gibson

Designed by Amanda Barlow
Edited by Jenny Tyler
Illustrated by Amanda Barlow
Photography by Howard Allman

I can draw...

a lion

1. Crayon the head.

2. Add two ears. Fill in with a felt pen.

3. Crayon a nose.

4. Add the mouth and two eyes.

5. Crayon a big bushy mane all around.

6. Add whiskers.

a cat

1. Crayon a round head.

2. Crayon a fat body.

3. Add two eyes and ears.

4. Crayon the nose and mouth.

The crayon will
show through.

5. Add some
whiskers, and
a tail.

6. Crayon stripes.
Go all over with
a felt pen.

a dolphin

1. Crayon a curvy line for the tummy.

2. Crayon another curve for the back.

3. Add a long nose.

4. Crayon a fin on
top and underneath.

5. Draw in an eye.
Add the mouth.

6. Crayon the tail.
Fill in with a felt pen.

7

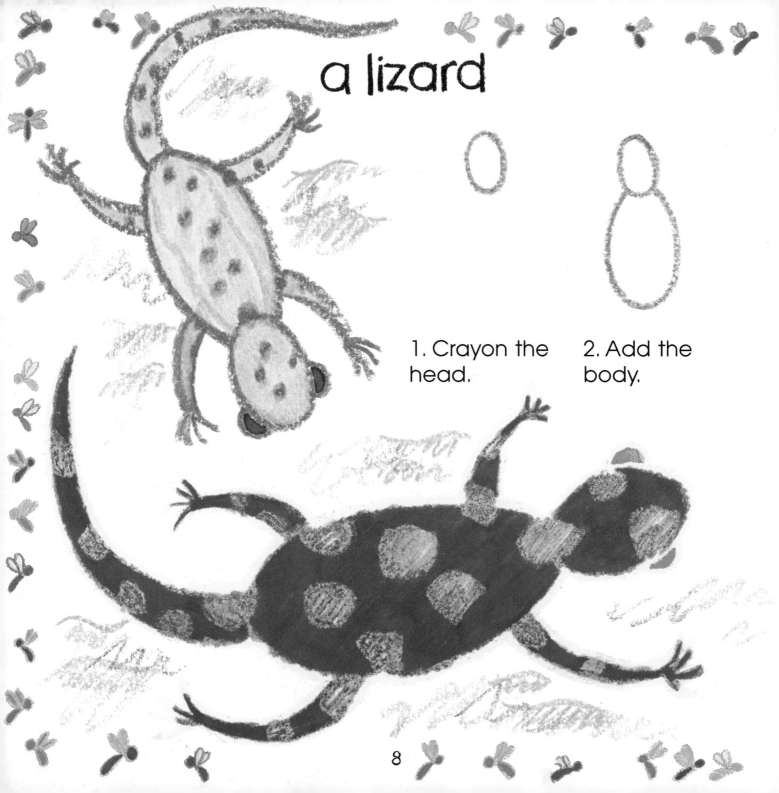

a lizard

1. Crayon the head.

2. Add the body.

8

3. Add the legs and eyes.

4. Add a tail and patterns.

5. Add toes. Go over with a felt pen.

9

a rabbit

1. Draw a round head.

2. Add two long ears.

3. Add the body.

4. Put in eyes and a nose.

5. Draw the mouth and tail.

6. Add whiskers. Fill in with a felt pen.

10

Draw some
lettuces like this.

11

a hen

1. Crayon a body.

2. Add the neck and head part.

3. Add a beak and eye. Crayon a tail.

4. Do striped legs. Crayon wing feathers.

5. Crayon the red parts. Go over your hen with a felt pen.

Draw some chicks like this.

a teddy

1. Crayon a head.

2. Add ears and a muzzle.

3. Put in the eyes, nose and mouth.

4. Crayon a fat body.

5. Add the arms.

6. Draw the legs. Fill in with a felt pen.

a tiger

1. Draw a face. Fill it in with a felt pen.

2. Put in the eyes, nose and ears.

3. Add fur around the face.

4. Crayon a long shape for a body.

5. Draw the legs and the tail. Fill in with a felt pen.

6. Crayon black stripes. Add claws and whiskers.

Draw some
flowers and
creepers like
these.

17

a fish

1. Crayon the body.

2. Add an eye and the mouth.

3. Crayon some patterns.

4. Go over with a felt pen.

5. Crayon a tail and two fins.

a monkey

1. Draw the head.

2. Add the body and a curly tail.

3. Add the muzzle and two ears.

4. Put in the eyes, nose and mouth.

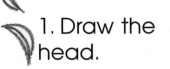

5. Do the arms and legs.

6. Add hands and feet. Fill in with a felt pen.

a frog

1. Crayon a body.

2. Add big eyes, a mouth and nose.

3. Crayon the front legs. Add toes.

4. Crayon the back legs. Add toes.

5. Crayon spots. Go over with a felt pen.

Draw leaping frogs like this.

a horse

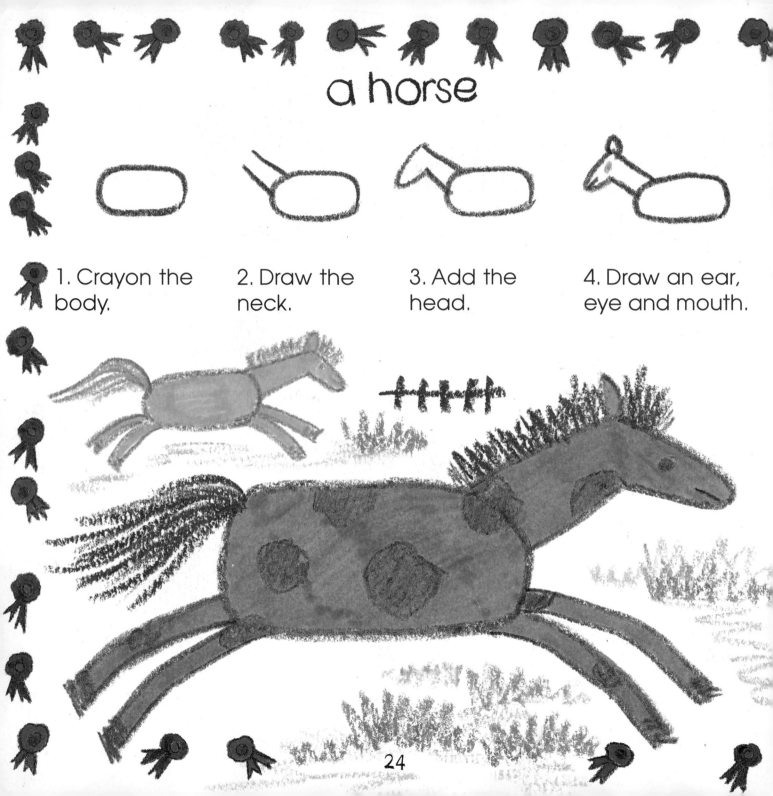

1. Crayon the body.

2. Draw the neck.

3. Add the head.

4. Draw an ear, eye and mouth.

5. Crayon four legs. Add the hooves.

6. Add a mane and tail. Fill in with a felt pen.

25

a turtle

1. Crayon a big, round shell.

2. Add the head. Put in the eyes and mouth.

3. Draw the front and back legs.

4. Add a tail. Crayon a pattern around the shell.

5. Crayon more patterns. Go over with a felt pen.
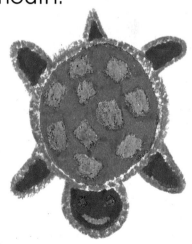

Add a sea
background

27

a flamingo

1. Crayon the body.

2. Add tail feathers and a neck.

3. Draw the head. Fill in with a felt pen.

4. Add a beak, an eye and feathers.

5. Draw long thin legs with knobbly knees.

6. Add the feet.

28

You could draw
your flamingo
standing in water.

a reindeer

1. Crayon the body. Add the neck.

2. Do the head. Add two ears.

3. Add four long legs and a tail.

4. Crayon hooves, a nose and two eyes.

5. Draw jagged antlers.

6. Add spikes to them. Fill in with a felt pen.

a bee

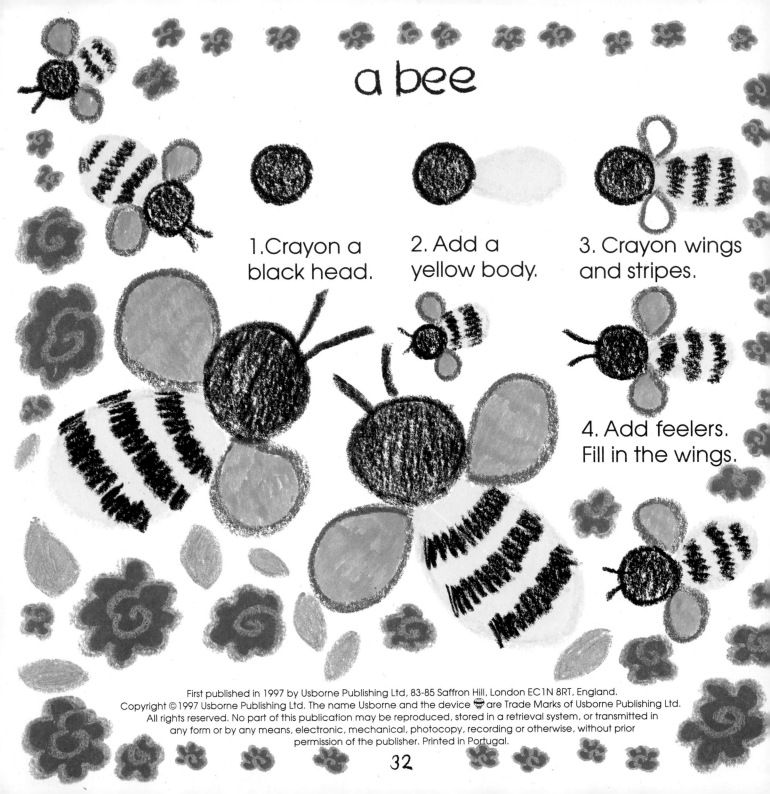

1. Crayon a black head.

2. Add a yellow body.

3. Crayon wings and stripes.

4. Add feelers. Fill in the wings.

First published in 1997 by Usborne Publishing Ltd, 83-85 Saffron Hill, London EC1N 8RT, England.